HEALING
AFTER DIVORCE

100 PRACTICAL IDEAS
For Kids

Also by Alan Wolfelt:

Healing a Friend's Grieving Heart:
100 Practical Ideas for Helping Someone
You Love Through Loss

The Journey Through Grief:
Reflections on Healing

Healing a Child's Heart After Divorce:
100 Practical Ideas for Families, Friends and Caregivers

The Wilderness of Grief: Finding Your Way

The Mourner's Book of Hope:
30 Days of Inspiration

Transcending Divorce:
Ten Essential Touchstones for Finding
Hope and Healing Your Heart

The Transcending Divorce Journal:
Exploring the Ten Essential Touchstones

Also by Raelynn Maloney:

Waking Up:
A Parent's Guide to Mindful Awareness and Connection

*Companion Press is dedicated to the education and
support of both the bereaved and bereavement caregivers.
We believe that those who companion the bereaved by
walking with them as they journey in grief have a
wondrous opportunity: to help others embrace and grow
through grief—and to lead fuller, more deeply-lived lives
themselves because of this important ministry.*

Companion
P R E S S

For a complete catalog and ordering information, write or call:

Companion Press
The Center for Loss and Life Transition
3735 Broken Bow Road
Fort Collins, CO 80526
(970) 226-6050
www.centerforloss.com

HEALING
AFTER DIVORCE

•

100 PRACTICAL IDEAS
For Kids

•

ALAN D. WOLFELT, PH.D.
RAELYNN MALONEY, PH.D.

Companion
PRESS

Fort Collins, Colorado
An imprint of the Center for Loss and Life Transition

Companion Press is an imprint of the
Center for Loss and Life Transition,
3735 Broken Bow Road, Fort Collins, Colorado 80526
970-226-6050
www.centerforloss.com

Companion Press books may be purchased in bulk for sales promotions, premiums or fundraisers. Please
contact the publisher at the above address for more information.

Printed in the United States of America

20 19 18 17 16 15 14 13 12 11   5 4 3 2 1

ISBN: 978-1-617221-38-5

A NOTE TO PARENTS AND OTHER LOVING GROWNUPS

This book is about grief and mourning. It's about the feelings kids have during and after a divorce and how to express those feelings and heal. We wrote this book for children ages 6 to 12 who are coping with the changes that come with divorce—changes in their families and their day-to-day lives. Each idea in this book is designed to help kids integrate their grief through mourning.

Kids grieve during divorce. That's because they lose something that they value—their family as they once knew it and everything that goes along with it. Maybe they lose their home, neighborhood, or school. Or maybe they lose the little things, like dad being available to play ball or mom to help with homework. Divorce brings many changes, large and small, and each change represents a loss.

In order to accept the divorce and move from a painful, insecure place to one that's more calm and stable, kids need to mourn. While it may seem like the best thing to do as parents is to distract your kids from their painful emotions, doing so only delays their healing. To heal from loss, people need to *mourn*—to release feelings of loss, anger, frustration, disappointment, and sadness. Mourning allows kids to move what's *inside* their hearts and minds to the *outside*. Doing so helps kids integrate the divorce and strip it of its power over their lives.

Grieving and mourning aren't easy work. It takes a committed, patient parent to allow a child to express his feelings in his own words and in his own way. It may take a long time, and it may feel like he is expressing the same feelings and desires over and over again. It may not always be comfortable, but when you give him permission to mourn you are allowing important work to happen; you are letting him move through grief and heal. He needs your support, love, and acceptance right now. And he needs it from other adults in his life, too.

Commit to going through this book with your child or the child you are supporting through divorce. If you can, make it a part of your routine to explore one of the 100 ideas and activities each day. Congratulate yourself for being a parent or significant adult who is willing to help a child mourn. It takes an aware person to acknowledge the grief that divorce brings. By helping the child mourn, you are giving her the gift of a happy, stable future in which she can engage in meaningful relationships and fully experience life's joys.

LET'S GET STARTED

Divorce is hard. Grownups do not always know how hard it is for kids. The grownups who love you want you to feel okay. Grownups want you to feel happy and enjoy your life. You are a kid, and kids are supposed to have fun. But kids do not usually feel happy about divorce.

Does it ever feel like nobody wants to talk about the divorce? Some grownups try to protect you by not talking about it. They think that if they don't bring it up, you won't think about it so much or feel bad about it. But that's not true. You probably think about it a lot right now, huh? Maybe you got the message from some people that talking about the divorce wasn't okay. But it is okay. In fact, it's good for you to talk about it. It's even good to cry, yell, or whine about it, if you need to.

Divorce can make kids feel sad, confused, frustrated, disappointed, and angry. Some kids have a lot of questions about divorce, like "Why is this happening to my family?" Maybe you are one of them.

Your feelings about divorce are called grief. Grief may be a word that you haven't learned yet. Don't worry, it's easy to understand. Grief is the mix of feelings you feel when you lose something that's important to you. It's what you feel when your grandma dies, when your pet dies, or when your best friend moves away. It is the painful thoughts and feelings you are having right now about your parent's divorce. Because of the divorce, you have lost your family as it has always been—everyone together under one roof.

Grief is a funny thing. It's like eating your least favorite food. Even if you don't enjoy it, the only way to get through the meal is to dive in. It's the same with your feelings about the divorce. Even though it doesn't feel good to feel sad or angry, it is the only way to feel better later on.

It helps to have someone who will listen to your feelings about the divorce and help you understand them. Talking about how you feel and whether you are mad, sad, or worried about the divorce helps get those feelings out. If you don't get them out, you will have them inside you all of the time, like a painful wound that won't heal. But if you let them out, your wound will scab over and begin to heal. It won't hurt as much.

Have you ever heard the word mourning? If grief were a face, mourning would be the mouth. When you mourn you talk, scream, cry, laugh, pout, and sigh to release your feelings. You need to mourn so you can feel better. If you don't mourn, your feelings will stay bottled up inside and get in the way of enjoying your family and friends, both now and in the future.

That is why we wrote this book. If you read the words and do the activities—and share this book with someone who loves you—you will get your feelings out rather than hold them in. You will feel better. We work with a lot of kids whose moms and dads are divorced. These kids have taught us a lot about grief and mourning. We have seen kids let their grief feelings out and feel happy and enjoy life again.

This little book has 100 ideas on what you can do to mourn. If you read it with your mom, dad, or another grownup you like, you'll get to share what you are thinking in your head and feeling in your heart. This book will also help grownups understand what divorce is like for you, which is really important.

We are sorry that you have to deal with this divorce. Divorce is hard. It brings lots of changes. We know that having to see your mom and dad separately is not easy. It is also no fun to have to move between houses or have your daily routine mixed up. But there are things to do that will make these changes easier, and doing the activities in this book will help.

While you go through your parents' divorce, you might feel mixed up. Know this: You are a great person. You are loved. You deserve to feel safe and happy. And you are going to make it through this divorce. We know this because we have seen lots of other kids do it. With the help of this book and the grownups who care about you, you will be able to mourn and get your feelings out. You will do great!

Alan Wolfelt   Raelynn Maloney

1.

LEARN ABOUT DIVORCE GRIEF.

- What is *grief*?

- The word grief rhymes with leaf.

- Grief is all of the things you feel in your heart, think inside your head, and feel inside your body about your parents' divorce. You might feel sad, mad, confused, scared, unsure, or worried. Your tummy might hurt, or it might be hard to fall asleep.

- When you have grief you are grieving (a word that rhymes with leaving).

Write or draw what you think your grief looks like here.

2.

LEARN ABOUT MOURNING.

- What is *mourning?*

- Mourning sounds just like the word at the end of this sentence: "I eat breakfast every morning."

- The kind of mourning we are teaching you about is an action word like running or jumping. Mourning is the action of letting your grief thoughts and feelings come out.

- When you mourn you will feel better and this divorce will not be so hard. If you keep everything inside, you will not feel good because that means you are carrying your grief. You have to let all those painful feelings out. And you have to do it over and over again, until you don't feel them as much as you did before.

Write or draw what you look like when you are mourning.

3.

LEARN HOW GRIEF AND MOURNING ARE DIFFERENT FROM EACH OTHER.

- Grief is all of the feelings you feel on the inside about the divorce. You might feel sad or angry or confused or frustrated or tired or relieved.

- Mourning is letting your feelings out by talking, crying, laughing, complaining, drawing, dancing, running, and writing.

Write or draw what grief and mourning might say to each other if they were cartoon characters, monsters, or animals.

4.

BE NICE TO YOURSELF.

- Is the divorce one of the hardest things that has ever happened in your life?

- It is not easy to have so many things change all at once.

- Be nice to yourself during this divorce. Imagine that you are your own best friend.

- Some ways to be nice to yourself are:
    - Make a list of all of the things that are good about you.
    - Let yourself cry if you need to cry.
    - Take a nap when your body feels tired.
    - Think about all the things that you are good at or like to do.
    - Tell yourself that you are going to make it through this divorce!
    Remind yourself that your mom and dad love you very much.
    - Think of a friend who is special to you.

Write or draw something that shows you being nice to yourself.

5.

KNOW THAT THE DIVORCE IS REAL.

- Your family is getting a divorce. Divorce means that your parents are not going to stay married anymore. It also means that you are not going to all live together in the same place. That is hard to believe because living together may be the only way it's ever been.

- Some days you may not want to think about the divorce. You may even want to pretend it never happened. That's okay to do some days but not every day.

- It's hard to accept that your family is really getting a divorce. It is hard to believe that things will never be the same again. But it's true. If you can accept this, you will start feeling better. You will start to see that some of the changes the divorce brings are good.

Write or draw your feelings about the divorce being real.

6.

LET YOURSELF BE UPSET.

- Feeling sad or angry or upset is no fun. But it's okay to feel this way right now. Something really sad has happened in your life.

- You don't have to feel upset every minute, though. It's also okay to laugh and play and have fun. Think of play as your job as a kid.

- You will feel upset sometimes. You might feel itchy inside, like your feelings want to burst out. You might feel angry, scared, sad, or worried. Find a way to get these feelings out. You could draw, write, run around, build something, have a pillow fight—whatever feels right.

- Be sure you find a way to get your upset feelings out in a way that doesn't hurt you or anyone else.

Write or draw what you look like when you are upset.

7.

REMEMBER WHAT YOUR FAMILY WAS LIKE BEFORE THE DIVORCE.

- It's good to remember how it felt to be with your family before the divorce. Even though things are changing, you will always have memories of fun and happy times. You might also have memories of hard and stressful times.

- All of these memories are okay to have and to talk about. It's good to talk about what you remember to grownups who are good listeners.

- It might help to look at pictures of trips your family took together or special times you spent with your family when you were all together.

- If you feel like crying or laughing when you look at pictures, go ahead. This is another way to get your feelings out. Remember that letting feelings out means you are mourning.

Write or draw your feelings about your family before the divorce.

8.

UNDERSTAND THAT YOUR LIFE
IS DIFFERENT NOW.

- When families get divorced a lot of things change, big and little. What has changed for you?

- Divorce can change the way you spend your days. Your daily routine might be different now. Maybe you take the bus to school instead of getting a ride. Or maybe you come home to an empty house after school. What is different right now?

- When families change each person might have things that change about them, too. Know this: Your mom is still your mom. Your dad is still your dad. Yet your mom is not going to be a wife anymore and your dad is not going to be a husband.

- Your life will not be exactly the same ever again. That doesn't mean it won't be happy, it will just be different. Someday you will get used to the difference.

Write or draw your feelings about your changed life.

9.

ASK WHY.

- You might find that you are filled with questions. Questions like:
  - Why do grownups get divorced?
  - Why do families change?
  - What will happen after the divorce?
  - Why can't my parents just stay together?

- Pretend the divorce is a cave and go in and explore it. Look at the walls, the ground, the rocks, and the light. Exploring divorce will help you to understand it better and feel less upset about it later on.

- If you can, talk to your parents or another grownup about why this is happening. They might not have the answers, but talking about it helps.

Write or draw your feelings about exploring divorce.

10.

LET OTHERS HELP YOU WITH YOUR GRIEF.

- Grief is hard. You need people who love you to help when you have grief in your heart and in your head.

- Don't be afraid to let someone help you, especially grownups.

- If you need help and no one notices, it's okay to ask for help from your parent, teacher, aunt, or neighbor. Just say, "I need help with all of these feelings I am having." Or you could say, "This divorce is hard and I don't know what to do about it."

**Write or draw your feelings about
getting help from others.**

11.

FEEL NOTHING SOMETIMES.

- Has your foot or leg ever fallen asleep because you rested on it too long? At first it feels completely numb, then it starts to tingle and hurt.

- Your grief might feel like that, too. At first you might feel nothing. This is called feeling numb. It's okay to feel numb because soon you'll start to tingle and hurt. Try not to shove your hurt feelings back down. Let them come out a little at a time, even if they sting a bit.

Write or draw what numb feels like.

12.

PLAY TO GET GRIEF OUT.

- Even kids who feel grief like to play.

- Playing is what kids are supposed to do. Have fun playing every day.

- Sometimes grief escapes when we move our bodies.

- For example, you can get out mad feelings by playing kickball or sad feelings by playing with your stuffed animals.

Draw yourself playing games or doing activities that let out your grief.

13.

TALK TO GROWNUPS WHO ARE GOOD LISTENERS.

- It's important to find grownups to talk to about your grief.

- Think about the grownups in your life. Which ones make you feel safe and loved, and which ones are good listeners?

- Maybe you want to tell them your feelings or ask them questions. Kids usually have a lot of questions when their families get divorced. Grownups might not have the answers, but it's still good to ask the questions that are floating around in your head.

Make a list of the grownups who have good listening ears and talk with one today.

14.

TALK TO A FRIEND.

- Did you know that friends are there to share both good times and hard times?

- Your friends probably don't know what to say to you about the divorce. Some kids do not know what grief is and have never felt it, unless they have been through divorce or the death of someone they loved.

- Do you have a friend whose family is divorced? If so, ask your friend to tell you the story of the divorce. You might find that your friend feels some of what you feel. Share your story, also.

**Draw a picture of you and your friends
sharing your stories about divorce.**

15.

CRY WHEN YOU NEED TO.

- Crying is not only for babies or little kids. Crying is for everyone because everyone's eyes make tears.

- Do you think that it's okay to cry when your body gets hurt, like when you get a cut? It's also okay to cry when your insides get hurt, like when your life changes because of divorce.

- Crying helps your body let out its sadness, anger, hurt, and confusion.

- If you can, find a grownup who will hold you when you feel like crying.

What thing about the divorce makes you want to cry? Write or draw about it here.

16.

GET GOOD SLEEP.

- Grief can really tire you out. When things change we get tired more easily.

- When you are tired you might feel grumpy or you might have a harder time controlling your anger. You might get frustrated more easily than usual. You might have a hard time focusing on your schoolwork.

- Your body needs extra sleep right now. Go to bed early if you are feeling tired. Take a nap after school if you need to. It's okay to spend time relaxing and doing nothing.

How do you know when you are tired? Write or draw the messages your body sends you when you are tired.

17.

FEED YOURSELF GOOD FOOD.

- Grief can leave you feeling hungry. Your body needs good food like a car needs clean gas. Your body will feel better if you give it good food to fuel it right now.

- Sometimes when we have grief our body plays tricks on us: we don't feel hungry even when our body needs food or we can't sleep even when our body is tired. When our body is tricky like that, we have to make ourselves eat and sleep.

- Try to eat a good breakfast every morning even if you are not that hungry. Do you know what the four food groups are? They are grains, vegetables and fruits, milk, and meat and beans. Try to eat from each food group at least once a day and get at least five servings of fruits and veggies.

Make a list of your favorite healthy foods or draw them here.

18.

DRINK A LOT OF WATER.

- Besides good food and good rest, your body needs a lot of water right now.

- Did you know that over half of your body weight is water? Our bodies need water to work right.

- Get in the habit of drinking from a water fountain whenever you see one. Take a water bottle to school if your teacher says it's okay. Drink a big glass of water after school each day and another one after playing outside.

Draw a happy body that has plenty of water.

19.

RUN AROUND OUTSIDE.

- There's something about the outdoors that makes us feel better. The bright sun, blue sky, and wind in our faces feels refreshing and satisfying.

- Is it a nice day outside? If so, go outside and do something fun. Practice shooting baskets or kicking a ball in a goal. Jump on a tramp. Roll down a hill. Climb a tree. Play tag with neighbor kids. Go on a nature walk. Go to the park and slide or swing. Play in the sandbox.

- If the weather is not very nice, sit on the step and watch the rain come down or relax on the grass and count the clouds in the sky.

Draw a picture of you doing something you enjoy outside.

20.

FIND A GRIEF HIDE-OUT.

- Sometimes it's good to have a private spot to go to when you want to be alone with your grief or sad feelings. Do you have a special place to go? It could be a fort in your backyard, a favorite big tree or boulder, or a quiet place in your house.

- When you are in your grief hide-out, you can cry, write, draw, play, sing, dance, talk out loud, or just sit and think.

- If you want, hide some goodies there. If it is outside, put them in a Ziploc baggie. Gather up a notebook, journal, sketchpad, comic book, or snacks.

What cool things would you want to put in your grief hide-out? Make a list and show it to your mom and dad.

21.

DON'T BE ALONE TOO MUCH.

- If you want to be alone with your grief, that's okay to do sometimes. Go to your room or your grief hide-out to have time alone.

- But don't do it all of the time. It's good to be around other people, especially if they make you feel good inside. If you feel sad and want to be alone, try talking to someone who cares about you, instead.

Outline your hand with a pencil in the space below.
In each finger write the name of someone you can
call or spend time with if you are feeling alone.

22.

LET YOURSELF FEEL HAPPY.

- Just because something sad has happened in your life doesn't mean you can't feel happy.

- Do something every day that makes you feel good and smile. Watch a funny show, share a joke with a friend, or play a silly game.

- Having fun doesn't mean the sadness will go away. It just means that you are not letting the sadness be with you all of the time.

What makes you feel happy? Draw a picture of happy things.

23.

PLAY WITH A PET.

- Animals are comforting to be around. They are playful. They are always there when you need them. They are always happy to see you, and they love you no matter what.

- If you have a pet, spend some special time with it today. Give it a hug or a snuggle. Let it lick your fingers or chase you around the yard. Let its excitement make you excited.

- If you don't have a pet, visit a pet shop or play with a neighbor's pet so that you can have some animal time. Be sure to ask permission ahead of time.

Draw a picture or write a story about your pet or a pet that you like.

24.

GO TO CHURCH OR A PLACE OF WORSHIP.

- Does your family belong to a church or go to another place to worship? If so, going regularly will help you with your grief.

- Church often feels like a safe place. You might feel safe sharing what you are thinking and feeling with someone at church. Church can help you change your mood from sad to hopeful.

- Does your church have a youth group or a choir? If so, consider joining.

- If your family doesn't attend church and you want to go, ask them to take you sometime so you can see if it is something you might find comforting and helpful.

Draw a picture of church. Write about
what church means to you.

25.

WRITE IN A JOURNAL.

- Not everyone likes to write. If you like to write, a journal is a safe place to put your thoughts and feelings.

- Writing about what you are feeling can make you feel better. Writing about your grief is a great way to mourn.

- It's your journal so you can write as much or as little as you want. You decide what you want to write about and how often you want to write.

- You can write a letter to your parents about the divorce even if you never want to give it to them. You can write about the questions you have. You can write about what you are going to miss about your family being all together.

If you could design your own journal, what would the cover look like? Draw it here.

26.

DO ART.

- Do you like to draw, paint, color, make paper airplanes, or fold origami figures? Making art is another great way to mourn.

- You can photograph something outside, mold clay, paste together a collage, or build a sculpture. Try whatever sounds fun to you.

- As you do your art, try to express your grief in whatever you are making. Be creative!

Research art projects on the internet or in a book and make a list of ones that sound fun to you.

27.

WRITE A POEM ABOUT DIVORCE.

• Poetry is a great way to get your feelings out of your head and onto paper.

• It's fun to rhyme, at least some of the time. Try writing a poem about your family or about the divorce. Don't worry, it doesn't have to rhyme and it doesn't have to be a masterpiece.

• Try this fill-in-the blank poem to get you started:

Because of divorce my family is changing.

I feel _____ about all this rearranging.

If mom and dad only knew

that I think divorce _____ through and through

maybe they would not mind

If I said "_____" sometimes!

Write your poem here and decorate the margins with drawings and symbols. Share your poem with someone you like and trust.

28.

CRANK THE TUNES AND DANCE.

- Dancing feels great. Our bodies like to move to music. When we dance we often leave thoughts behind. Sometimes it is as if the music takes over our bodies and we just can't help but move them around.

- Music can help you heal. It can help you feel energy and lift your spirits when you are feeling down. It lets you act out your grief and get those strong feelings out.

- When you dance, think about the divorce. Let your body move and tell the story of how you feel, right now.

Who is your favorite singer? What is your favorite song? Draw a picture of you dancing here.

29.

PLAY YOUR FAVORITE SPORT.

- Are you playing a sport right now? If so, that's a great way to burn off some of the energy that the divorce is making you feel right now. If you are not, think about a sport or activity you have always wanted to try and ask a parent to help you sign up.

- Some kids say they are "allergic" to sports, mostly because they haven't found one that they like. Remember, there are a lot of activities besides the usual ones like soccer, baseball, and football. Consider something funky like rock climbing, gymnastics, or yoga.

- Sports keep your body healthy and are a great way to make friends and learn new skills.

What sports do you like to play? What sports don't you like to play? Make a list of each and circle the sport you love the most.

30.

PLAY A BOARD GAME.

- What board games are in your closet? Do you have Monopoly or Connect Four? Have you ever played chess or checkers? Do you have a favorite card game, like Crazy 8s or Go Fish?

- Board games are a great way to take a break from all your feelings and to just have fun.

- Ask your brother, sister, or friend to play a board game with you today.

If you could plan a play date with a friend today or tomorrow, who would you choose? Make a list of the things you like to do with this friend.

31.

WRITE A LETTER TO YOUR PARENTS.

- Is there anything you wish you could say to your parents that you are afraid to say?

- It's okay to have questions for your parents and to tell them how the divorce makes you feel. Sometimes it's easier to know what you are feeling if you write it down first.

- You can read the letter to your parents, or you can read it to another grownup you like and trust.

- It's also okay to keep the letter tucked away in your room and read it later to yourself.

Write about or draw a picture of something you want your parents to know about divorce.

32.

MAKE A FAMILY MEMORY BOOK.

- Memory books are scrapbooks filled with memories of your family. They help you feel better when you are missing your family and the way it used to be. They also help remind you that your family is still your family.

- Gather things that remind you of your family, like photos, drawings, ticket stubs, birthday cards, programs, or anything else. These are called mementos.

- Get a blank journal or make a book yourself by folding several sheets of copy paper in half. Make a cover out of colored paper or the inside of a cereal box. If you want, cut out pictures or words from magazines that remind you of your family.

How does looking at all the mementos of your family make you feel? Write or draw about it here.

33.

DRESS UP LIKE SOMEONE ELSE.

- When something hard happens, people sometimes wish they were someone else. Do you ever wish you could be someone else? Maybe you would like to be someone in your class at school or a character in a book?

- It could be that what you really want is your life to be easy and less stressful again—and someone else's life might look that way to you.

- It's okay to pretend you are someone else for a couple of hours. Play dress up if you want. Pretend to be another real-life person or an imaginary one. Enjoy pretending for an hour or two. This will give you a break from your grief.

If you could be anyone in the world, who would you be and why? Draw a picture of you as this person.

34.

KEEP A FAMILY TREASURE.

- When you were smaller you might have had a special blanket or teddy bear that made you feel safe.

- It's okay to keep things that make you feel good. If you want, dig out your old blanket or stuffed animal. Or find something else that belonged to you when your family was living together. Your treasure could be the key to your old house, a rock from the backyard, or a souvenir from a trip.

- Choose something that reminds you of happy times together. If it's small enough, bring it back and forth between your mom's house and your dad's house.

**Draw a picture of a special time that
you had with your family.**

35.

PLANT A GARDEN.

- Do you have a place where you can plant flowers or vegetables?

- Digging in the dirt can be a lot of fun.

- It's amazing to watch a tiny seed grow into a tall sunflower or a super-long zucchini.

- It feels good to grow things. Just like flowers, trees, and vegetables, you and your family will keep growing and changing, too.

What kinds of things would you like to plant in a garden? Draw them here. If you were a flower or tree, what would you look like? Draw it here, too.

36.

TELL YOUR FRIENDS AND FAMILY YOU LOVE THEM.

- Maybe this big change has made you realize how special certain people are to you.

- People love to hear that you care about them. Tell your special people that you love them, today.

- Do something nice for them for no special reason.

Draw a heart with a note and show it to someone you love.

37.

HUG SOMEONE TODAY.

- It's amazing how much better you can feel just by hugging someone you love.

- Hugs can help you feel safe. Hugs remind you that you are loved.

- Hug your parents or your sibling or a friend or your teacher. Hug your pet. Just hug!

Finish this sentence. I wish _____ was here to hug me. I like hugs because they make me feel _____ _____.

38.

BE A FRIEND TO SOMEONE ELSE WHO IS GOING THROUGH DIVORCE.

- Do you know anyone else who has parents who are divorced or are getting divorced?

- If you do, be especially nice to that person this week.

- You could say, or give them a card that says, "I know that your parents are divorced. Mine are getting a divorce, too. I know what you are going through!"

- Maybe the two of you can even talk about feelings together.

What do you and other kids you know think about divorce? Write your answer here.

39.

MAKE A GIFT FOR SOMEONE SPECIAL.

- Has anyone ever told you this saying, "It's better to give than to receive?"

- It feels good to give gifts to others. It feels especially good to give gifts as a surprise when there isn't any special holiday or reason to give a gift.

- Giving gifts is a way to say something without words. When you give a gift it's like saying:
    - I'm thinking of you.
    - I love you.
    - I think you are great.
    - I care about you.

- The gift doesn't have to be something you buy. A gift can be a picture that you draw or color, a poem that you write, or a stuffed animal or toy that you no longer want but you know someone else would like to have.

Draw a picture of you giving a gift to someone you care about. How does the gift make that person feel?

40.

MAKE A ROCK TREASURE BOX.

- Collect five or six rocks from a park, your yard, or a trail you hike. Find nice flat ones in colors that you like.

- Take a permanent marker (with your parent's permission) and write words on the rocks that remind you of divorce. Some of the words might be CHANGE or BLAH or ANGER or OKAY or ANNOYED.

- Whatever words you choose are the right words.

- Put these rocks in a little box so that when you are thinking about the divorce you can read them or add more words on the other side.

Write or draw how you feel about this.

41.

BE WHO YOU ARE.

- When parents get divorced certain things change. You might be living in a different house, or you might see your parents on different days. Maybe the way you feel when you wake up each day has even changed.

- This divorce has changed your life and your feelings, but a lot of things about you have not changed. You are still the same person you were before the divorce. If you were shy, you are probably still shy. If you were silly, you are probably still silly.

- If you are silly, you might handle your grief in a silly way. That's okay. If you are shy you might find it hard to talk about your grief. That's okay, too.

- It's good for you to handle your grief in a way that feels right to you.

Draw a picture of yourself here. What are you thinking and feeling in this picture?

42.

SING LOUDLY.

- Do you like to sing? Do you have any favorite songs or a favorite singer that you like?

- Music can make us feel different feelings. It can help us feel hard feelings like sadness or anger. It can also help cheer us up when we are feeling down.

- Singing loudly helps us let those feeling out.

- Find a song or CD that you like and crank it up (with your parent's permission).

- Sing in the shower. Sing and dance around your bedroom. Sing in the car.

- You don't have to have a great singing voice, just the courage to use it!

What are some of the lyrics to your favorite song? Write them here.

43.

TELL A GROWNUP WHEN YOU ARE UPSET.

- When you are upset, it's best to tell someone why.

- Do the adults in your life know when you are upset? How do you let them know that you are having a lot of strong feelings?

- Adults don't always notice when kids are feeling down, sad, or upset. Sometimes kids have to tell them exactly what they are thinking and feeling for them to help.

- It's okay to tell an adult things like, "I'm feeling unhappy." Or, "I'm mad about all of this." And, "I'm tired of going back and forth between houses."

- Your parents might feel like they have to fix your problems. Sometimes things can't be fixed, but it helps to tell someone how you are feeling anyway. You can say, "I don't need you to fix how I feel, I just need you to listen."

- If your parents don't have time to listen, find another grownup who does.

Draw a megaphone and write the words that you would most like to say to someone about your upset feelings.

44.

LISTEN TO YOUR BODY.

- Our bodies have a great way of telling us when they are feeling stress.

- If you are tired, cranky, or have a lot of stomachaches, your body might be trying to tell you that you are stressed.

- Talk to a grownup about stress and how it affects your body.

- Find a way to relieve your stress so that your body doesn't have to carry so much of it around. Things that can help include relaxing on the couch, jumping rope, dancing, or being outside on a sunny day.

Draw an outline of a body. Now, put a big red dot on the places that hurt, ache, or feel uncomfortable. What do you think these sore spots are trying to tell you?

45.

GIVE YOUR GRIEF A FACE AND A NAME.

- Did you know that everyone's grief is different? Your sister might feel grief as sadness, while your brother might feel it as anger. Then it could switch around. Your mom's and dad's grief are different, too.

- No one else will think exactly like you think or feel exactly what you feel.

- Your grief is special, just like you.

- Draw a picture of your grief. Imagine it as a creature or person. What does it look like? What is its name? Ask your parents or brothers and sisters to do the same. When you are finished, talk about how everyone's grief looks different.

What color is your grief? Be sure to color your picture of grief.

46.

PACK A FAMILY KEEPSAKE BOX.

- Get a shoebox or another box with a lid. The box can be as big or as small as you want.

- Decorate the box with stickers, paper, paint, or markers.

- Gather things that remind you of your family.

- Fill it with things like pictures of family vacations, a photo of your family home, old birthday cards, books your parents used to read to you, special videos like your parents' wedding day, DVDs you watched as a family, a magnet from your family refrigerator, or a deck of cards you all used to play with.

**Make a list of things you would like
to put in your memory box.**

47.

LIST THE PEOPLE YOU LOVE.

- Your parents are getting divorced, or they have already gotten divorced. Divorce is hard for kids.

- Always remember that even though this is happening, all of the people you love are still here with you. They will be here to laugh with you, take care of you, and love you for many, many years.

- This love will help you through this hard time.

- You also have friends and other grownups who love you.

Write a list of people you love and who love you here.

48.

TALK TO YOUR BROTHER OR SISTER ABOUT THE DIVORCE.

- If you have brothers or sisters, know that they have been hurt by this divorce, too.

- It's good to talk with them about your feelings and about how they are feeling. Spend time hanging out and playing together. Be gentle and understanding with each other.

- If you're fighting a lot with them right now, it could be because of the divorce. Grief can make people upset and grouchy.

- Do something to let your brothers or sisters know that you love them. Make a card or tell them you love them, today.

Write about or draw a picture of your brother or sister here.

49.

TALK TO A GROWNUP.

- Do you have grandparents or family friends who are older? Do you have a teacher you trust?

- They have been around a long time. They probably know many people who have gone through divorce. Talk to them about your grief.

- If they don't live nearby, write them an email or call them on the phone. Let them know if you are having a hard time at school, with friends, or at home because of your grief.

- Ask them to help if other kids are teasing you about the divorce.

What would make it easier for you to talk to a grownup about your feelings? Write or draw your ideas here.

50.

DON'T ESCAPE WITH VIDEO GAMES OR TV.

- It's tempting to watch a lot of TV, especially when you feel bad.

- TV shows and video games take your mind off of what is happening in real life. It's okay to do these things sometimes.

- But watching too much TV won't make your feelings go away. Your grief will wait for you to return. It will wait a long time, even until you are an adult. It will wait until it gets a chance to come out.

- If you put your feelings away until later, they get bigger rather than smaller.

- You can let your hurt out by telling people how you feel, writing about it, or expressing it in another way like doing art, playing, running around, and crying.

Draw a picture of a TV set hypnotizing you
here, with your grief growing inside of you.

51.

READ A BOOK.

- Have you read a good book lately?

- Storybooks are a good way to relax for an hour or two.

- Relaxing is a good thing to do when you are going through something like divorce.

What is the very best book you have ever read?
Write the name of it here and write why you liked
it so much or draw your favorite characters.

52.

BE A BIG BABY.

- When you are grieving it's okay to do things that seem babyish.

- It's natural to want to cry, be held, snuggle with grownups, or hug a stuffed animal.

- It's okay to do these kinds of things. They help you get your grief out and feel safe.

- If your parents tell you to stop, remind them that this is what helps you feel comforted and it won't last forever.

Draw a big, loud crying baby here.
What do babies need when they are upset?

53.

THINK ABOUT TIMES YOU DID THE WRONG THING.

- Sometimes when kids feel grief they misbehave.

- Misbehaving is one way kids try to tell adults that they are hurt or angry or confused.

- When we go through hard times, like divorce, our feelings can get mixed up and get too big for us to handle. We might say and do things that our parents see as bad.

- If you've been acting badly, talk to a grownup about it. Tell them how you feel about your actions and why you think you have been acting that way. Maybe the grownup can help you find a way to handle your feelings that won't get you into trouble.

What happens when you get into trouble for behaving badly? Draw or write about it here.

54.

PUT A PICTURE OF YOU AND YOUR PARENTS IN YOUR ROOM.

- It's good to look at pictures of your family and to remember all the special times you had together.

- Find a cool frame and ask a grownup to help you put a picture of your family in it to keep in your bedroom.

- If you want, get a small frame, key chain, or locket so you can carry it with you. It could go in your school backpack or the duffle bag you bring back and forth between houses.

- Remember, even though your parents are divorced, you are still a family.

What is your favorite photo of you and your parents? Where were you when the photo was taken, what were you doing, and what did you feel like that day? Write about or draw that memory here.

55.

ASK FOR HELP AT SCHOOL.

- Divorce can be stressful for kids. Sometimes when you are stressed it's hard to stay focused at school.

- It can be hard to work on reading, math, or science when all you can think about is the divorce. It can be hard to pay attention to what your teacher is saying.

- If your grief or something about the divorce is making school a little harder for you right now, talk to a grownup about it.

- Talk to your parents, a relative, a friend's parent, or a teacher. Ask them to help you make a plan for getting back on track at school.

Draw or write about what is hard for you
at school right now. Has this always been
hard, or did the divorce make it hard?

56.

JOIN A DIVORCE SUPPORT GROUP FOR KIDS.

- Did you know there's a place you can go to sit and talk to other kids about divorce?

- Talking to other kids who have divorce grief can feel good. It feels good to know you are not the only one whose parents are getting a divorce.

- You'll also make friends and get some good ideas on what to do when you feel angry, sad, and frustrated.

- Ask an adult to help you find a kids' support group. A good person to ask is your mom, dad, or the school counselor.

- With permission, go online to find out about groups in your city. The website DivorceCare for Kids at www.dc4k.org can help you find a group near your home.

Write a list of questions you would like to ask other kids who are going through divorce.

57.

TALK TO A COUNSELOR.

- Talking about grief to grownups who care about you is always a good idea.

- Counselors go to school to learn how to help kids with divorce. Counselors are people who've helped other kids through hard times like divorce, school problems, friendship problems, and more.

- If your parent or teacher suggests you see a counselor, give it a try. The counselor will help you feel better about all the changes in your life. The counselor will help you figure out how to feel less worried, stressed, or upset. If you are having trouble sleeping, he or she will help you with that, too.

Make a list of things you would like to talk to a counselor about, or questions you have about counseling. Start by writing what you are sad, mad, scared, or worried about when it comes to the divorce.

58.

DON'T BE SURPRISED BY *GRIEFBURSTS*.

- Sometimes out of nowhere you will feel a sudden wave of sadness that you didn't expect. This is called a griefburst. Griefbursts might make you want to cry.

- Everyone who experiences grief gets griefbursts.

- Griefbursts can be scary, surprising, or embarrassing. They come when you don't expect them—when you are at recess, at the grocery store, watching a movie, or spending time alone in your room.

- When you have one it helps to tell a grownup about it. If you don't feel like talking, it's okay to just snuggle up with someone you love and sit quietly until it passes.

What do you think a griefburst looks like? Have you had any griefbursts about the divorce? Draw your picture here.

59.

EXPECT GRIEFBURSTS ON SPECIAL DAYS.

- Griefbursts, or feelings of grief, will probably pop up on certain days that are special to you and your family.

- Days like your birthday, your parent's birthday, Christmas, and Halloween can be hard after a divorce.

- They are hard because they might be different than what you were used to when your family was all together. Plus, both of your parents might not be there this year.

- Ask a grownup who cares about you to spend time with you on these days.

- Talk about how it was before and how it has changed.

- Think about what would make it better and share your ideas.

Draw or write about your favorite special days. Is one coming up soon? Be sure to draw your grief somewhere on the page so that you remember it might be there on those days.

60.

DO SOMETHING THAT YOU LOVED
TO DO WITH YOUR FAMILY.

- Even if your family doesn't do certain things together anymore, like going to the park for a picnic, that doesn't mean you have to stop doing these things, too.

- What did you do together that you loved to do? Did you go bowling? Ride bikes? Go sledding? Have a movie or game night? Take hikes? Go to baseball games?

- You can still do all of these things even if one parent is not there.

- Think of something you used to do and do it today by yourself, with a parent, or with a brother or sister. Ask a grownup to do it with you if it's something you can't do yourself.

Draw a picture of you doing an activity with your family. Ask a parent when you can do this again.

61.

FIGHT THE URGE TO BE STRONG.

- Don't try to be strong and fight off your grief. You might think strong people never cry or show a lot of emotion.

- Did you know that it is brave to show your emotions, even the hard ones?

- Don't try to stuff your grief inside.

- Let others know what you are really thinking and feeling. Find safe people to share your grief with. Sharing grief takes honesty.

- Remember, mourning means letting your grief out. You will have to let it out again and again until it doesn't hold power over you anymore.

- When you mourn you are being strong because mourning is hard work.

Draw a picture of yourself mourning here.

62.

NEVER HURT YOURSELF OR OTHERS.

- Hurting yourself or someone else never helps how you are feeling. It might feel good for the split second you do it, but then it will feel bad for a long time.

- Your life might feel hard right now with all of the changes, but it will get better. As time goes by and you keep letting grief out, you will start to feel less upset and more stable, like a tree with deep roots. Little things won't shake you up anymore.

- People love you and want you to feel better. They are here to help you and to listen to you.

- If you are having scary thoughts about hurting yourself or someone else, talk to a grownup you trust right away. You will feel better.

Draw or write about any scary thoughts you are having. If these thoughts were monsters, what would they look like?

63.

LIST WHAT'S GOOD ABOUT YOUR LIFE.

- Sometimes when we are feeling grief and sad things are happening, we forget about the good things in our lives.

- Even though your parents are getting divorced, there are good things that are also going on in your life.

- What do you like about your life right now? What is fun? What makes you happy? Who brings you joy? Think about both the big and little things.

- Feeling thankful for the good things in our lives is called having gratitude, or feeling grateful. When we feel grateful we feel peaceful inside.

**Make a list or draw five things you
are grateful for right now.**

64.

APPRECIATE YOURSELF.

- Did you know that you are an awesome kid?

- Think about all the reasons that you are spectacular, amazing, and cool.

- Mainly you are great because you were born into this unique family and they love you very much. Some people in your family might be feeling upset right now, but they still love you even when they are upset. Even when they don't show their love, they feel it.

- Your family and the world just wouldn't be the same without you!

- Reach your hand over your neck and give yourself a pat on the back, just for being you.

Draw or write about something that makes you a great kid.

65.

FEEL WHAT YOU FEEL.

- Everyone in your family is grieving the divorce. But your grief is not like everyone else's. The way you think and feel about the divorce is different than how your parents, brother, sister, or friends feel about the divorce.

- Grief can change every day. You might feel sad and lonely one day and okay the next.

- It's okay to feel whatever you feel, even if it's different than your parents. Maybe you feel sad. That is okay. Maybe you feel mad. That is okay too. Some kids feel scared because they don't know what is going to happen in the future. Some kids feel relieved or happy because there is less fighting in the house. None of your feelings are wrong or bad. They just are.

Draw a circle below and color it to show how you feel about the divorce. Use red to show anger. Use yellow to show happiness. Use black to show sadness. Use any other colors that speak to you.

66.

JOIN A CLUB.

- Getting involved in a club or new activity might really help you feel better right now.

- It's good for you to be around kids who are laughing and having fun.

- Would you want to join the Girl Scouts or the Boy Scouts? Do you have a 4-H club nearby? Is there a local soccer team or karate club you want to join? Ask your mom or dad if you can try a new activity and sit with them and page through the catalog of your city's recreation department.

If you could join a club or do an activity, what would you choose? Draw a picture of a few possibilities here.

67.

DON'T LET ANYONE TAKE AWAY YOUR GRIEF.

- Sometimes adults want kids to stop grieving.

- That's because they don't want you to feel sad or upset.

- But you have the right to feel your grief and to show your feelings, even if it's hard for grownups.

- If someone says you shouldn't feel the way you do, don't believe it. If someone says, "It's not that big of a deal," don't believe it. If someone says, "You are being a big baby" because you are showing your feelings, don't believe it.

- Instead, choose to talk to someone who will let you express your grief. These are the grownups who are the best helpers.

Draw or write about a time when a grownup tried to take away your grief.

68.

IF YOU ARE A BOY, KNOW THIS:

- Sometimes grieving boys are told they have to be strong and act like a man. They might be told that they have to now be the "man of the house."

- If one of your parents has left the house, you might feel pressured to grow up too quickly and take over adult jobs, like making dinner, watching your siblings, worrying about grocery shopping, or getting the trash out on time. But you are still a kid! You're not a man yet.

- You still need lots of help with your grief and all the other regular kid-things going on in your life.

Draw or write about why it is important for you to be a kid right now instead of trying to be the man of the house.

69.

IF YOU ARE A GIRL, KNOW THIS:

- Sometimes grownups expect girls who are going through a hard time, like divorce, to cry and be sad all the time. If you're not feeling sad today, that's okay. It's okay to play and have fun. You don't have to be sad if that is not what you feel.

- Sometimes girls are expected to take over chores at home when one parent leaves, like watching younger siblings or making meals. It's good to help out around the house, but remember that you're just a kid. You shouldn't have to take care of brothers and sisters too much or cook and clean too much.

Draw or write about why it is important to be a kid and not be a little adult.

70.

MAKE A WISH.

- Close your eyes and wish for something you really want.

- Lots of kids wish that their parents would get married again, that their parents would be kind to each other more often, or that they wouldn't fight about the parenting schedule in front of them. If you want this, that's okay. It might not happen, but it is okay to wish for it.

- Your parents are not likely to get back together, but maybe you have another wish that's really possible!

- What do you wish for? Wish your wish. Now, figure out how to make it happen.

**Write down or draw three wishes you have
about the divorce or your life right now. Share
these with a grownup who cares about you.**

71.

HELP YOUR FAMILY MOURN.

- Sometimes grownups are not very good at mourning.

- Your family might have to learn how to mourn.

- Encourage the people in your family to talk about the divorce. Tell them there are no strings attached or expectations. Tell them you just want to talk about it. It's good to talk about the divorce together, once in a while.

- Share memories of when you were all living under the same roof and spending time together. Talk about how divorce has changed your family.

**Draw or write about how your family
gets their grief feelings out.**

72.

HAVE A SLEEPOVER.

- Get permission from your parents to invite a friend or two to sleep over this weekend.

- It's good for you to be around friends right now.

- Sleepovers can be a lot of fun because you can play games, watch movies, eat popcorn, tell jokes, and be silly together—all things kids should do.

- If there's a chance to talk about the divorce and your feelings with your friend, do it. Friends are there for fun but also for caring.

Draw or write about the friends you will invite for a sleepover if your parents say yes.

73.

WRITE A STORY.

- Once upon a time there was a kid who was feeling _____ because his or her parents decided to get divorced.

- Make up the rest of this story and write it down.

- Later on, read your story to a grownup who loves you.

- Read your story again in a few months to see how it sounds. See if it feels different and if you would change the story in any way.

Write your story here and give it a title.

74.

DON'T LET OTHER KIDS GET TO YOU.

- Lots of kids don't know how to talk about hard things, like divorce.

- Some kids might even tease you or say mean things.

- Mostly kids act this way because they are scared. They are scared that maybe divorce will happen to them if they spend time with someone who is going through it.

- It's silly, we know, but some kids don't know that divorce is not something you can catch, like a cold.

- Find a friend who understands and won't hurt your feelings when you talk about your grief feelings.

Write or draw a picture of what you can do if a friend does or says things to hurt your feelings.

75.

ASK A GROWNUP TO TEACH
YOU SOMETHING NEW.

- What have you always wanted to learn to do?

- Juggle? Cartwheels? Whistle through your fingers? Skateboard?

- It is fun to learn something new, especially when you are feeling stressed about things happening in your family.

- If you know someone who is good at something cool, ask them to teach you how to do it. If a grownup isn't around, practice something new with a friend, brother, or sister.

- Trying new things brings a smile and laughter into your life. It's fun to taste a food you haven't tasted before, like fondue. It's exciting to go to a place you've never been before, like the skate park. It's fun to learn a new skill, like rollerskating.

- What is something you would like to try?

Draw a picture of you doing something new that you'd like to learn. How does it feel to learn something new?

76.

IF YOU ARE FEELING MAD, TRY THIS:

- You might feel mad that your parents are getting divorced or have already gotten a divorce.

- When we are mad we feel like there's a boiling hot pot of water inside that's making us feel hot and red inside. Sometimes you might feel like you are going to explode.

- It's okay to feel mad or angry about divorce, but it's not okay to hurt anyone or anything when you have these feelings.

- Instead, try to get your anger out in safe ways. Scribble with crayons really hard on a piece of paper. Draw an angry face and words that tell how you feel inside. Jump rope as fast as you can or scream into a pillow to get your mad feelings out.

How can you get your mad feelings out? Write two ideas here:

77.

IF YOU ARE FEELING SCARED, TRY THIS:

- Sometimes divorce makes kids feel afraid. Even grownups feel afraid when divorce happens.

- When we are afraid our tummies can hurt or we might feel all jittery inside, like we want to run away or hide.

- The best thing to do when you are feeling afraid is to talk to someone about your fears or write a story about them to share with a grownup.

- Find someone to tell. Say, "I'm scared because _____ _____."

Draw what you look like when you have scared feelings.

78.

IF YOU ARE FEELING GUILTY, TRY THIS:

- Sometimes kids feel guilty about the divorce. Guilt is a heavy, yucky feeling that makes you feel like you did something wrong, even when you haven't.

- Maybe you feel like you caused the divorce somehow. You didn't! The divorce is between your mom and your dad. Period.

- It's normal to feel these feelings, but you didn't do anything wrong. Divorce is something that parents choose, not something kids do!

- Talk to your parents or another grownup about any guilty feelings that you feel.

**Write about or draw yourself or someone
else having guilty feelings.**

79.

IF YOU ARE FEELING RELIEVED, TRY THIS:

- You might feel relieved about your parents getting divorced. Maybe your parents argued or fought a lot when they were living together. No kids like to hear their parents fight!

- Feeling relieved makes you want to say, "Whew! Glad that's over!" and give a big sigh.

- Maybe you have mixed-up feelings about the divorce. Maybe you loved the family together but didn't like how it felt when you all spent time together. Maybe once you wished that they'd get a divorce and now you wish that they hadn't.

- You might feel lots of different feelings at once—scared, worried, sad, mad, confused, and relieved.

- It's okay to feel relieved or mixed up about your parents getting a divorce. Many kids have these same feelings.

**Draw or write about feeling relieved now that
your parents are no longer together.**

80.

LOOK AT THE SKY.

- Take some time to lie on your back in the grass, on the deck, or on a lawn chair and look at the sky.

- Did you know that watching the sun and clouds can make you feel peaceful and calm?

- The same is true about watching the stars and planets at night. It can make you feel like you are a part of something really important. And you are.

- Look at the night sky and imagine what is out there. Or imagine creatures and shapes that you see in the clouds. It will take your mind off your own life for a little while.

Draw or write about yourself looking up at the sky, during the day or night. How do you feel? What do you see?

81.

GET A DREAM CATCHER.

- Do you know what a dream catcher is? A dream catcher is a small net shaped around a circle. It is often made of leather and sometimes has designs on it. Native Americans made them to block out bad dreams and catch good ones. You can find them in gift stores.

- If you have trouble sleeping or have bad dreams, a dream catcher can make you feel better. You can hang it by your bed or on your bed frame.

- Some Native Americans believe that when the sun shines on a dream catcher in the morning, it burns bad dreams away.

- If you can't buy one, make one. Do an internet search on "How to make a dream catcher." Go to to www.youtube.com and find a video about how to make a dream catcher. Ask a grownup for help.

**Aren't dreams funny and weird? Draw or
write about a dream you had recently.**

82.

KEEP A CALENDAR.

- When parents get divorced, kids usually start to live in two different places. They have a home with mom and a home with dad

- Keeping track of all of this can be tough. It's nice to know when you are going to see mom again or be at dad's house in advance. Keeping track on a calendar helps.

- Ask your parents if you can buy or make a special calendar that has all these days marked clearly. Maybe dad's days are yellow and mom's days are purple. It might help to know what time you are going to be picked up each day by your parent, too.

- You can even put other events and holidays that you look forward to on this calendar.

Draw the homes you live in, now that your parents are divorced.

83.

COOK WITH YOUR MOM OR DAD.

- Some kids love to cook and bake. Do you?

- Ask one of your parents or another grownup to cook with you. It's fun to cook and make something yummy to eat.

- While you are cooking, talk about how you are doing and how things are going at home.

- Maybe you can make a special meal that you have always enjoyed with your family or bake a special treat for the parent you are not with right now. This will help you feel close again, even if you can't all eat it together.

Draw yourself cooking or baking something delicious. What are your favorite foods to make? Draw them, too.

84.

PLAN A CEREMONY.

- Have you ever been to a wedding or watched someone graduate? These are called ceremonies, and they are what we do when something big happens in our lives.

- Something big is happening in your life right now that is causing big changes. Why not plan a ceremony that recognizes these changes?

- Ceremonies don't have to be big events that a ton of people attend. They can be simple.

- Maybe you can light a candle and say something important or make a collage with pictures of your family and keep it on your bookshelf. You could also go to a special place that your family enjoys, like a park or a favorite nature trail, and sit on a bench and make a wish or say a prayer.

- Call this your "My Family is Changing" ceremony. Invite friends—and your mom and dad, of course!

Think about a ceremony that you'd like to do. Draw a picture of it or write about it. What could you do to let everyone know that something big is happening in your family?

85.

ASK QUESTIONS.

- When divorce happens, kids have a lot of questions:
    - Why do parents get divorced?
    - Will my mom still be my mom? Will my dad still be my dad?
    - What will happen now?

- Sometimes kids are afraid to ask their parents these questions. It's okay to ask questions.

- If your parents do not want to answer your questions, or don't have answers, it's okay to ask another grownup. Find a grownup who is a good listener and who will help you find your own answers to these questions.

Make a list of questions you have about the divorce.

86.

TALK ABOUT YOUR PARENTS' NEW FRIENDS.

- After parents get divorced, they sometimes meet new people.

- Someday, your mom or dad might introduce you to a new friend. They might even call their new friend a boyfriend or girlfriend.

- It's good to share with your parents how you feel about any new friends that they have in their life.

- If you feel like they are spending too much time with their new friends and it bothers you, tell them.

- Let them know that you miss spending time with them and that you also need some alone time with them right now.

Draw or write about how you feel about any of your parents' new friends.

87.

EXPECT CHANGE.

- When parents get divorced things change—schedules change, rules change, and even where you live can change.

- Change happens all of the time. Change can be good but it can also be hard.

- There are books that teach you about how to cope with change. Ask your parents to help you learn about the process of change. Go to the library and check out books on change.

- Change happens. It is something that you will get used to.

**Draw or write about how the divorce has
changed what you do every day.**

88.

GATHER FAMILY PHOTOS.

- Pull out old family photo albums or ask your mom and dad if they can help you find photos of the family.

- It's a good idea to keep pictures of your family around. They are fun to look at, and they help you keep important memories in your mind and in your heart.

- If you discover several loose photos, put them in a book or pick your favorite ones to put in a frame. Keep the book or framed pictures in your room, so you can see them often.

- Ask your parents to look at photos with you so you can talk about your memories together.

Draw or write down the memories you have about one of the photos

89.

WRITE A LETTER TO "DIVORCE."

- Is your parents' divorce new to you? Do you know what divorce means?

- Kids have lots of ways of explaining divorce. Some kids have told us divorce is when mom and dad stop fighting. Another child told us that divorce is when mom and dad live in two houses. A few kids have said that divorce is when mom and dad don't like each other.

- What do you think divorce is?

- Whatever it is, pretend that you are writing a letter to Divorce. Maybe your letter will ask questions of Divorce or express mad or sad feelings toward Divorce. The letter can say whatever you want it to. Here is an example:

Dear Divorce:

I think you are _____. When my mom and dad told me about you I felt _____.
Why did you come into my family? I wish you
_____.

From, Me

Ask your parents to answer your letter to Divorce.

90.

KEEP FAMILY RITUALS.

- Is there something that you do every day? Brushing your teeth in the morning? Reading before bed? Watching cartoons on Saturday mornings? Cooking eggs with your mom or dad for breakfast?

- A ritual is when we do something over and over again. Sometimes we do it every day. Other times we do it once a year, like when we celebrate a holiday.

- Families have rituals like eating together, going to the park every weekend, watching a show together, or having a family game night.

- After divorce, these rituals might change. If you like the old rituals and want to keep doing them, tell your mom and dad. It's important to keep some things the same after a divorce.

Draw or write about one of your favorite family rituals

91.

USE THE WORD GRIEF.

- Now that you know what the word grief means, go ahead and use it. Let your parents know it's okay to use the word grief.

- Lots of people don't realize that divorce causes feelings of grief.

- That's funny, because everyone who goes through divorce feels grief.

- Don't pretend that divorce feels okay when it doesn't. You can say, "I feel my grief feelings right now. I feel _____."

Draw or write the word grief. Think of words to describe your grief that begin with "g," "r," "i," "e," and "f."

92.

DRAW A BEFORE-AND-AFTER PICTURE OF YOUR FAMILY.

- Draw a line down the middle of a blank piece of paper.

- On one side draw a picture of your family one year ago.

- On the other side draw your family today.

- Are the pictures the same? How are they different? What's changed? How does everyone feel in each picture?

If you could change one thing about the divorce, what would it be?

93.

COLOR.

- Coloring can help when you are stressed or having a hard time.

- Sometimes coloring hard and fast is a good way to get feelings out. Sometimes coloring soft and careful helps you feel calm inside.

- You can use crayons, markers, colored pencils, or chalk to color.

- Spend some time coloring in a coloring book, using chalk on the driveway, or making a big picture or poster. You can also ask your parents to find a special type of art called a *mandala* on the internet that you can color any way you like.

- There is no right way to color. Only your way.

- Give your work of art to someone, put it in your journal, or throw it away. It is up to you.

Make a list of things you'd like to draw or color.

94.

PRAY.

- When people pray they make wishes about their lives and other people's lives. They make important statements about their lives.

- Some kids have learned to pray when they are not feeling their best. They find that it makes them feel better.

- If you know how to pray and it feels good to you, it's okay to pray about what is happening with the divorce.

- If you don't know how to pray but want to learn, ask a grownup to teach you.

- There are lots of different ways to pray. You can cross your hands or not. You can get on your knees or not. You can close your eyes or not. You can talk out loud or not. Pick a way that feels right to you.

Draw yourself praying or write about what you might pray for.

95.

DO SOMETHING SILLY.

- Don't forget that you are a kid! Kids love to be silly and goof off.

- Isn't it the best to have a water balloon toss or a squirt gun fight? What about jumping on a trampoline, playing tag on the playground equipment, or making a silly video with friends?

- Goofing off lets us laugh and forget about our troubles. It lets us get out feelings of stress and worry.

- Who do you like to goof around with? Ask your mom or dad if you can set up a play date with your favorite silly friend, today.

Make a list of your favorite silly people and write or draw what you like to do with them.

96.

PLAN A TRIP.

- You need a lot of time with both of your parents right now. Ask your mom or dad if you can go on a short trip—camp out for a night, visit a relative, or go to a hotel, if possible.

- Going on a trip is great because parents spend time hanging out and playing with you rather than doing work or chores around the house.

- Sometimes when we get out of the house and stay somewhere else, we see our lives in a new way.

- If you can't get away overnight, see if you can spend a whole day somewhere else, like exploring a nearby town or national park.

If you could go on a trip, where would you go? Write about or draw it here.

97.

MAKE YOUR MOM AND DAD A CARD.

- Make a card for each of your parents that tells how you feel about them and talks about the changes your family is going through right now.

- Draw a picture. Write a poem. Decorate it with glitter or jewels. Use a collage of pictures and words from magazines in your card.

- Whatever type of card you make, know that your parents will like it. Everyone loves to get home-made cards. It will also give your parents the important message that the divorce is something that's okay to talk about.

Draw a picture of you giving your special card to your mom and dad.

98.

GO FOR A WALK WITH EACH
OF YOUR PARENTS.

- Divorce usually means you have less time with one or both of your parents.

- It also probably means that you are running around a lot, and you feel like you are always on the go.

- It's important to slow down and have time with each of your parents.

- Ask one of your parents to go on a walk with you today. It's a good way to spend time together that's not hurried or rushed. Walk around the block or to a nearby park. Bring the dog. Ride scooters or bikes.

Draw a picture of you taking a walk with one of your parents. How do you feel, and what are you two talking about?

99.

PLAY TRUTH OR DARE.

- Sometimes it is hard to talk about our true feelings. It can be easier when we turn it into a game, like truth or dare.

- Tell your family that you'd like to play truth or dare.

- Follow these rules:

    - People have to tell the real truth and anyone can ask anything they want about the divorce.
    - People must give an honest answer, but they have a right to tell their truth in a way that is safe for them. They can tell details or hold them inside.
    - Dares have to be silly, fun things, like daring someone to dance with the family dog or run around the house.
    - The game must stay positive and not be used as a way to hurt each other, only as a way to be honest with each other and kind to each other.

- After the game, talk more about what came up. Ask questions and give each other hugs and smiles.

In a game of truth or dare, what questions would you ask the people in your family? Write about it here.

100.

KNOW THAT SOMEDAY YOU WILL FEEL BETTER.

- You'll never stop missing having your family together, even though sometimes it will feel just fine when you are not all together.

- Someday it won't hurt every time you think of the divorce.

- As time goes by you won't feel so sad about it, especially if you talk about how it feels to have divorce in your life.

- When you get feelings out, you make more room for happiness to get in. Getting feelings out is called mourning. Re-read number 2 in this book if you forgot what mourning means.

- Over time you'll probably think about the divorce less often, too. That's okay. It doesn't mean you wanted the divorce, it just means that you are learning to live with it.

Write or draw about a happy time that you imagine in your future.

A FINAL WORD

Did you enjoy this book? We hope so. Did it help you understand your feelings about the divorce? Mostly, we hope that you've learned how important it is to mourn—to let your grief out.

If you have grownups and friends around to help you mourn, you will get through this. You'll never completely get over the divorce. You will always miss the family you once had. But as you mourn and let your feelings out over time, you will discover that the divorce doesn't hurt like it once did. You will find that you are happy and that you can have fun and enjoy life.

Like a flower after a hard spring rain, you're probably feeling battered right now. The flower needs sun and the gentle tending of a gardener. Find special grownups in your life to be your gardeners. Maybe it's your mom, dad, aunt, grandma, coach, teacher, or school counselor. These grownups can give you the love and help you need to heal the wounds that you have from the divorce.

When you get the help you need to heal, you will open up wide, like a sunflower opens to the sun.

We would love to meet you someday. We know you could help us learn more about what it's like to be a kid going through divorce. We know you could help us help other kids.

We wish you the best as you move through your divorce grief and get to the other side.

MY GRIEF RIGHTS DURING
AND AFTER DIVORCE

1. I have the right to have my own unique feelings about the divorce.

2. I have the right to talk about my divorce grief whenever I feel like talking.

3. I have the right to show my feelings of divorce grief in my own way.

4. I have the right to get help from other people with my divorce grief, especially grownups who care about me.

5. I have the right to get upset about normal, everyday problems.

6. I have the right to have griefbursts about the divorce.

7. I have the right to pray for God to help me with my divorce grief.

8. I have the right to ask why my parents got divorced.

9. I have the right to talk about memories I have of my family.

10. I have the right to feel all the feelings of divorce grief over time and at my own pace.

GLOSSARY OF TERMS

Ceremony

Events or actions we take to mark when something important is happening in our lives. Big ceremonies are weddings, graduations, and baby showers. Small ceremonies are putting flowers on a grave or lighting advent or Menorah candles. Ceremonies are created by our culture, but we can create our own ceremonies to mark important events or happenings in our own lives, too.

Change

Something that happens after big life events. Change causes things to be different from what they were before. When divorce happens, there are many small and large changes.

Counselor

Someone who helps people understand their feelings during times of change or loss. They help people when they are confused or unsure of what to do about something that is happening in their lives. They help people, including kids, grieve, mourn, and feel better.

Divorce

A legal word—used by lawyers and judges in the court of law—that means the end of a marriage. When two people get married, they get a license that says they are married. A divorce ends that license. Divorce also means that a family that was once all together now lives apart and that parents who were once a couple are no longer a couple. Divorce does not ever change the fact that you are your parents' son or daughter.

Grief

The thoughts and feelings you have on the inside when a big change happens in your life that feels hard or you lose something you value. You feel grief when someone you love dies, when you have to move and you don't want to, and when your parents get divorced.

Griefburst

Sudden strong feelings of sadness. Griefbursts are normal but they can be really hard. They can make you cry or want to run and hide. If you have a griefburst, let a grownup know how you are feeling.

Mourning

Letting your grief out by talking about it, writing or drawing about it, playing it out, crying, or doing activities that help you think about the divorce.

Rituals

An action that is repeated over time. Rituals are like ceremonies. They are used to mark special occasions or events. Rituals can be well-planned out or more spontaneous and made up. Examples of rituals include things we do to celebrate holidays, like putting gifts under the tree at Christmas, going to church on Easter, getting Easter baskets, and giving chocolates and hearts on Valentine's Day. We also have daily rituals, like reading a book before bedtime, catching the school bus, or calling mom or dad to check in.

Support group

A group of people who get together to talk about similar experiences. Divorce support groups for kids bring kids together to talk about what it's like to be in a divorced family. Support groups help you mourn. They also help you know that you are not alone. You can even make friends at support groups.

WANTED:
HEALING AFTER DIVORCE IDEAS

Please help us update the next edition of this book!

If an Idea is particularly helpful to you, let us know. Better yet, send us an Idea you have that you think other kids might find helpful. When you write to us, you are "helping us help others" and inspiring us to be more effective grief companions, authors, and educators.

Thank you for your help. Please write to us at:

Center for Loss and Life Transition
3735 Broken Bow Road
Fort Collins, CO 80526
Or email us at DrWolfelt@centerforloss.com or go to this website, www.centerforloss.com.

My idea:

_____

_____

_____

_____

_____

My name and mailing address:

_____

_____

_____

ALSO BY ALAN WOLFELT

Transcending Divorce

Ten Essential Touchstones for Finding Hope and Healing Your Heart

After years of being encouraged to contribute a book on divorce loss, Dr. Wolfelt has responded with this compassionate new guide. When it comes to grief and loss, divorce is one of the most heartbreaking for many people.

With empathy and wisdom, Dr. Wolfelt walks the reader through ten essential Touchstones for hope and healing. Readers are encouraged to give attention to the need to mourn their lost relationship before "moving on" to a new relationship.

If you're hurting after a divorce, this book is for you. Warm, direct and easy to understand, this is a book you will not want to put down.

ISBN 978-1-879651-50-0 • 195 pages • softcover • $14.95

Companion
PRESS

All Dr. Wolfelt's publications can be ordered by mail from:
Companion Press
3735 Broken Bow Road
Fort Collins, CO 80526
(970) 226-6050
www.centerforloss.com

ALSO BY ALAN WOLFELT

The Transcending Divorce Journal
Exploring the Ten Essential Touchstones

For many people, journaling is an excellent way to process the many painful thoughts and feelings after a divorce. While private and independent, journaling is still the outward expression of grief. And it is through the outward expression of grief that healing begins.

This companion journal to *Transcending Divorce* helps you explore the ten essential touchstones for finding hope and healing your grieving heart after divorce. Throughout, you will be reminded of the content you have read in the companion book and asked corresponding questions about your unique grief journey. This compassionate journal provides you with ample space to unburden your heart and soul.

ISBN 978-1-879651-54-8 • 134 pages • softcover • $14.95

Companion
PRESS

All Dr. Wolfelt's publications can be ordered by mail from:
Companion Press
3735 Broken Bow Road
Fort Collins, CO 80526
(970) 226-6050
www.centerforloss.com

ALSO BY ALAN WOLFELT

The Wilderness of Divorce

Finding Your Way

This hardcover gift book is a compassionate, easy-to-read guide to finding your way through the wilderness of divorce. This book is an excerpted version of the comprehensive *Transcending Divorce: Ten Essential Touchstones*, making it a more concise, friendly guide for the newly divorced.

ISBN 978-1-879651-53-1 • hardcover • 128 pages • $15.95

Companion
PRESS

All Dr. Wolfelt's publications can be ordered by mail from:
Companion Press
3735 Broken Bow Road
Fort Collins, CO 80526
(970) 226-6050
www.centerforloss.com

ALSO BY ALAN WOLFELT

Healing A Child's Heart After Divorce

100 Practical Ideas for Families, Friends and Caregivers

by Alan D. Wolfelt, Ph.D. and Raelynn Maloney, Ph.D.

How do you help children whose parents are separated or divorced? While divorce represents a significant loss for children—a loss that creates all the many natural feelings of grief, the children can continue to thrive if they are helped in these 100 practical ways by the caring adults in their lives.

ISBN 978-1-61722-142-2 • softcover • 128 pages • $11.95

Companion
PRESS

All Dr. Wolfelt's publications can be ordered by mail from:
Companion Press
3735 Broken Bow Road
Fort Collins, CO 80526
(970) 226-6050
www.centerforloss.com

ALSO BY ALAN WOLFELT

Living in the Shadow of the Ghosts of Grief
Step into the Light

Reconcile old losses and open the door to infinite joy and love

"Accumulated, unreconciled loss affects every aspect of our lives. Living in the Shadow *is a beautifully written compass with the needle ever-pointing in the direction of hope."*
— Greg Yoder, grief counselor

"So often we try to dance around our grief. This book offers the reader a safe place to do the healing work of "catch-up" mourning, opening the door to a life of freedom, authenticity and purpose."
— Kim Farris-Luke, bereavement coordinator

Are you depressed? Anxious? Angry? Do you have trouble with trust and intimacy? Do you feel a lack of meaning and purpose in your life? You may well be living in the shadow of the ghosts of grief.

When you suffer a loss of any kind—whether through abuse, divorce, job loss, the death of someone loved or other transitions, you naturally grieve inside. To heal your grief, you must express it. That is, you must mourn your grief. If you don't, you will carry your grief into your future, and it will undermine your happiness for the rest of your life.

This compassionate guide will help you learn to identify and mourn your carried grief so you can go on to live the joyful, whole life you deserve.

ISBN 978-1-879651-51-7 • 160 pages • softcover • $13.95

Companion
PRESS

All Dr. Wolfelt's publications can be ordered by mail from:
Companion Press
3735 Broken Bow Road
Fort Collins, CO 80526
(970) 226-6050
www.centerforloss.com

ALSO BY RAELYNN MALONEY

Waking Up

A Parent's Guide to Mindful Awareness and Connection

by Raelynn Maloney, Ph.D.

This practical parenting guide by Dr. Raelynn Maloney helps you become the parent you have always wanted to be—one who is present, aware, and connected. Complete with a series of simple Awareness Practices that help you cultivate self, relationship, and moment awareness, *Waking Up* will help you respond to your child in a healthy way and, in the process, help her learn the value she brings into relationships with others.

In *Waking Up* you will discover how to:

- develop and consistently use awareness as an effective parenting skill.
- transform "problems" in the parent-child relationship by first transforming yourself.
- actively prevent the passing-down of negative relationship patterns.
- shift your child's mood, attitude, and behavior by focusing on the relationship instead of the child.
- become aware of the messages your child is taking in from you -- and to avoid sending back negative or mixed messages.
- become grounded in the present with your child — and to raise a child who is also capable of being grounded in the present.
- transform difficult situations and ordinary experiences into mindful moments.
- stay connected to your child during disagreements, when giving consequences, or while setting limits.

Imagine parenting without losing yourself in the drama, the debate, and the tug of war. Interact with presence, openness, and confidence. Demonstrate the skills, habits, and mindsets that will positively influence your child for life.

ISBN 978-1-61722-146-0 • softcover • 224 pages • $18.95

Companion
PRESS

All Dr. Maloney's publications can be ordered by mail from:
Companion Press
3735 Broken Bow Road
Fort Collins, CO 80526
(970) 226-6050
www.centerforloss.com